FRANCIS FRITH'S

DID YOU KNOW? NOTTINGHAM

To Mum

Happy Birthday

Sam, Jake & Tim

THE FRANCIS FRITH COLLECTION

www.francisfrith.com

Did You Know?

NOTTINGHAM

A MISCELLANY

Compiled by Julia Skinner

With particular reference to the work of Douglas Whitworth

THE FRANCIS FRITH COLLECTION

www.francisfrith.com

First published in the United Kingdom in 2005 by The Francis Frith Collection®

This large print edition published in 2017 by Black Horse Books,
an imprint of The Francis Frith Collection
ISBN 978-1-84546-905-4

British Library Cataloguing in Publication Data

Did You Know? Nottingham - A Miscellany
Compiled by Julia Skinner
With particular reference to the work of Douglas Whitworth

The Francis Frith Collection
19 Kingsmead Business Park, Gillingham
Dorset SP8 5FB UK
Tel: +44 (0) 1722 716 376
Email: info@francisfrith.co.uk
www.francisfrith.com

Printed and bound in Great Britain

Front Cover: **NOTTINGHAM, LONG ROW EAST 1902** 48326p

The colour-tinting is for illustrative purposes only, and is not intended to be historically accurate

AS WITH ANY HISTORICAL DATABASE, THE FRANCIS FRITH ARCHIVE IS CONSTANTLY BEING CORRECTED AND IMPROVED, AND THE PUBLISHERS WOULD WELCOME INFORMATION ON OMISSIONS OR INACCURACIES

CONTENTS

INTRODUCTION

Nottingham is now very large, with a population of over 250,000, but it is also a very fine city with an historic core of great interest and quality.

The area is believed to have been originally settled by the charmlessly-named 'Snot' or 'Snota'. Place names ending in '-ingham' are early Anglo-Saxon ones, and excavations have revealed evidence to back this up on the eastern of the two hills on which the city stands. Snot's settlement later became a burh on the same hill – the word is still in use today as 'borough'. Following the Norman Conquest in 1066, William Peverel erected a castle on Tower Rock. The middle and upper baileys sit on the summit of the 130ft-high rock. It was a naturally impregnable site, with towering cliffs on two sides, and it dominated the country around, including the main road north, which crossed the River Trent below. The castle was steadily added to over the years, and its walls were rebuilt from 1068 onwards. From the mid 12th century it was an important royal castle, and in the 1470s it acquired grand state apartments in the middle bailey. King Charles I raised his standard at Nottingham Castle in 1642, the first action of the Civil War, although he soon left the city, which was strongly pro-Parliament. After the war the castle was 'slighted', or rendered useless, by the Parliamentarians, and was reduced to a ruin.

In the Middle Ages Nottingham prospered as a wool-dealing and cloth-making centre, and the River Trent was a vital trade artery. In the 18th century framework-knitting and bobbin lace took over, and these trades also spread to surrounding villages and towns. In later centuries Nottingham became famous for leather, textiles, engineering, tobacco, bicycles and Jesse Boot, the founder of the chain of chemist shops. The innovatory tradition is continued by the University of Nottingham, which has been in the forefront of some important research and technological achievements of recent years, including the development of the first genetically modified tomato.

Nottingham's story is full of colourful characters and events, of which this book can only provide a glimpse.

NOTTINGHAM, THE MARKET 1890 22807

NOTTINGHAM DIALECT WORDS AND PHRASES

'Throng' or 'thronged' - *very busy, as in 'the town was throng today'.*

'Kaled' - *delayed, held up.*

'Mardy' - *moody, crying, whingeing, as in 'a mardy child'.*

'Snap'- *food taken to eat at work.*

'Snap tin' - *the food container.*

'Clemmed' - *can mean either very cold, or very hungry.*

'A ya masht miduck?' - *have you made a pot of tea?*

'Corsey' - *pavement.*

'Jitty' - *an alleyway between houses.*

'Rammel' - *rubble, rubbish.*

'Derby road' - *cold, as in 'It's Derby road', it's a bit cold.*

'Laruped' - *covered with, ie 'laruped in mud'.*

HAUNTED NOTTINGHAM

It was at Nottingham Castle that the young King Edward III trapped his mother, Queen Isabella, with her lover, Roger Mortimer, and created one of the castle's most popular and enduring legends – the story of Mortimer's hole. This was supposed to be a cave leading from the cellars of Ye Olde Trip to Jerusalem pub to the castle, through which Edward III crept to capture Mortimer, who was later put to death. Mortimer's ghost is reputed to haunt the cave.

The Salutation Inn has been the scene of many strange happenings over the years, from pint glasses moving along the bar to levitating ashtrays and glasses falling off the shelves for no obvious reason, often 'floating' some distance away from the shelves before smashing on the floor.

There have been several reports of strange happenings at Wollaton Hall. Many attendants at the Hall have felt the temperature suddenly drop, or been aware of a hostile presence, often accompanied by the sound of a door slamming, footsteps, creaking floorboards and groans, particularly in Room 19, now used as an exhibition area. Investigations have found that Room 19 was where Lady Middleton was confined in her later years, in great pain after an accident in which she fell down some stairs. The area outside the Hall also seems to be haunted, as strange lights have been seen around the dovecote and the stable yard, and the ghost of a woman walking her dog has sometimes been seen around the lake.

NOTTINGHAM MISCELLANY

Magnetic resonance imaging scanners (known as MR scanners) were pioneered by Professor Peter Mansfield in the 1970s in the department of physics at the University of Nottingham. MR scanners are now used in hospitals throughout the world as a vital diagnostic tool. Professor Mansfield was knighted in recognition of his achievement, which has undoubtedly saved or prolonged thousands of lives.

Two of Nottingham's most famous entrepreneurs were Jesse Boot and John Player; the former developed a health empire, and the latter did his best to counter it by manufacturing billions of cigarettes.

The Normans established a new town, the 'French Borough', between the castle and the old Anglo-Saxon burh, the 'English Borough'. The present large market square was the heart of the French Borough. The heart of the old English Borough is the area around St Mary's Church, High Pavement and the Lace Market.

NOTTINGHAM, ST PETER'S CHURCH 1890 22834

NOTTINGHAM, CHEAPSIDE 1890 22821

Cheapside derived its name from the Old English word 'cepe' meaning bargain. The building to the right of Beecroft's in the photograph above was the Tudor home of the Earl of Mansfield. All these buildings were pulled down to make room for the new Council House in the 1920s.

After the canal arrived in the 1790s the population of Nottingham shot up, from about 11,000 in 1750 to around 60,000 in 1850. This was the period of the notorious 'courts' of tenements, crammed into any bits of field owned by speculators.

Unveiled amid great pomp in 1905, the year before the photograph below was taken, Albert Toft's then gleaming fresh marble statue of Queen Victoria was moved to the Memorial Gardens on Victoria Embankment in 1953, to make way for road widening. Its place has now been taken by a modern bronze family of four. In the foreground a woman is choosing from the pots laid out on the Stones, the traditional site of the pot market, where goods were laid out on straw.

NOTTINGHAM, THE QUEEN VICTORIA STATUE, MARKET SQUARE 1906 56462

The flamboyant hotel dominating this photograph was built in 1887 by the somewhat quirky Nottingham architect Watson Fothergill. Its lease expired in 1969 and its weirdly over-the-top architecture was swept away, to be replaced with a modern

development. The flags in this view are flying to celebrate the end of the Boer War.

NOTTINGHAM, THE BLACK BOY HOTEL, LONG ROW 1902 48326

NOTTINGHAM, THE POULTRY OR CHEAPSIDE, LOOKING TOWARDS MARKET SQUARE 1890 22822

Virtually everything in this view has been rebuilt since the photograph above was taken. The fine range of buildings on the right, some medieval, and those including Smith's Shoe booth which backed onto the old Exchange were all swept away to make room for the much grander 1920s Council House building with its shopping arcades.

Jesse Boot, one of Nottingham's most famous sons and a great benefactor to the city, started life in his widowed mother's herbalist shop, and went on to found the Boot's Pure Drug Company in 1888. The company is still the leading private employer in the city.

The great Central Railway arrived in Nottingham in 1900 amid much fanfare, and its station, Victoria, cost a princely £1million to build. The station was demolished to make way for the Victoria Centre in 1967, leaving only the tower intact as a sop to Nottingham's history.

James Hargreaves was one of the founding fathers of the Industrial Revolution. His Spinning Jenny machine mechanised the spinning of yarn for weavers, speeding up the production process; before mechanisation, it was said that a handloom weaver could need up to 16 spinners to supply him with yarn. Ironically, although his invention helped the mill-owners of Britain to achieve great wealth in the 18th and 19th centuries, James Hargreaves himself died in poverty in a Nottingham workhouse in 1777.

NOTTINGHAM, THE MARKET 1890 22808

The vast stone building of the Free Library in South Sherwood Street, designed by Lockwood and Mawson in correct decorated gothic style, opened in 1881 as the first home of the University College and the public library. Now a key part of Nottingham Trent University, it is surrounded by other campus buildings. Only the spire has gone since 1890.

Originally the main crossing of the River Trent from the south, the present elegant cast-iron Trent Bridge dates from 1871 and was designed by the Corporation Engineer, Marriott Ogle Tarbotton. It replaced the medieval bridge, which was in danger of collapsing. For a while the old and new bridges stood side by side, and Nottingham folk would talk of 'going down to the bridges' for long after.

In the 17th century the remnant of Nottingham's castle was given to the Duke of Newcastle, who had the upper and middle baileys cleared and levelled in order to build himself a ducal palace. Completed in 1679, after the Duke's death, the palace appears as austere as a prison block from a distance, but more ornamented when seen from a closer viewpoint. The building became a natural focus of resentment locally, and was sacked and burnt out in 1831, when Nottingham's outraged citizens learned that the Duke of Newcastle had voted against the Great Reform Bill. Eventually the ruin was taken over by the town and restored as a museum, which opened in 1878 as the first Museum of Fine Art in England outside of London.

NOTTINGHAM,
THE ROMAN CATHOLIC CHURCH 1890 24718

NOTTINGHAM, WHEELER GATE 1902 48327

Reputedly founded in 1189, the famous Ye Olde Trip to Jerusalem Inn claims to be the oldest in England. The present buildings are 17th-century at the earliest, with an 18th-century taller left bay. The Inn incorporates cellars cut into the sandstone of Castle Hill. The name possibly derives from the fact that the inn was built on the site of an old brewhouse where travellers to the Holy Land stopped for ale.

By 1924 the increase in traffic necessitated the widening of Trent Bridge and this was undertaken at a cost of £130,000. During the Second World War a temporary Bailey Bridge was stored for use in the event of Trent Bridge being bombed.

In 1895 a great frost which lasted for several weeks caused the river to freeze over completely. Fires were lit on the ice and skating was enjoyed by many people.

NOTTINGHAM, THE VICTORIA EMBANKMENT STEPS 1920 69443

The bulk of the medieval castle, largely made a ruin by the Civil War, was 'slighted', or made useless by order of Parliament in 1651. Now only the outer bailey east walls and a 14th-century

NOTTINGHAM, THE CASTLE GATEHOUSE 1890 22843

gatehouse survive. This photograph shows it in poor condition prior to being restored.

NOTTINGHAM, THE CASTLE GATEHOUSE 1920 69431

The 14th-century castle gatehouse was drastically restored in Victorian times, which unfortunately took away a lot of its character (see photograph on page 20). A small amount of the original old stonework can be seen in the archway and at the foot of the right-hand tower.

Built in 1863 in Italianate style by local architect Frederick Bakewell, and now part of Nottingham Trent University, Nottingham's School of Art was intended to train designers for Nottingham's lace industry. The ornate stone building now has 1960s brick buildings framing it to left and right.

North of the School of Art, the Arboretum was laid out in 1852. The Chinese Bell is in fact Russian: together with the four cannon it was seized as spoils of the 1854-55 siege of Sebastopol during the Crimean War.

The Dr Tate's Asylum in Ransom Road was built in 1857-59 by T C Hine. It was named after the medical superintendent who served here for the first 54 years of its existence. This asylum later became the Coppice Hospital.

During the brief reign of King Richard III, Nottingham Castle was the king's principal residence, and thereafter the great tower which he had completed was known as Richard's Tower. In 1485 King Richard III rode out of his 'Castle of Care' to the Battle of Bosworth Field, where he lost his crown - and his life. This battle saw the end of the Plantagenet line, and the beginning of the new Tudor dynasty, under the victor, Henry VII.

The photograph on page 23 looks across the lake to the pristine new Portland limestone of Morley Horder's Trent Building. Started in 1922, its classical design set the university's building style until the 1960s. The university college was founded in 1877, but did not achieve fully independent degree-conferring status until 1948. 1928 (the year of this photograph) was the year in which this building was opened by George V. Sir Jesse Boot, who donated the land and financed the building, was unable to attend the ceremony due to his disabilities, but afterwards the king and queen took tea with him.

NOTTINGHAM UNIVERSITY, THE TRENT BUILDING 1928 81572

NOTTINGHAM, WOLLATON HOUSE 1928 81579

The tide of Nottingham's expansion has now swept round Wollaton House (above), one of the great Elizabethan houses. Designed for Robert Smithson for Sir Francis Willoughby, who made his fortune from coal, it was built in the 1580s and is set in 500 acres of park. The land was bought by the Corporation in 1925.

Several trades for which Nottingham was well known in the past are perpetuated by street names, such as Pilcher Gate, named for the makers of 'pilchers', or furs, and Fletcher Gate, the street of 'fleshers' or butchers.

Beneath Nottingham's streets is a network of over 400 man-made caves, which visitors can explore on The Caves of Nottingham tour.

The County Cricket Club was founded in 1841, but the grandstand, or pavilion, which still remains, was almost new when this photograph (below) was taken. Six years later Trent Bridge staged its first test match against Australia. England was captained by W G Grace in his last test. Trent Bridge is one of the five cricket grounds in the country where Test Matches are played.

NOTTINGHAM, TRENT BRIDGE CRICKET GROUND AND GRANDSTAND 1893 33250

Jesse Boot gave money to landscape this area (below) as public gardens with Wallis Gordon's great archway and colonnades as a focus. The triumphal arch of the War Memorial, with its splendid green-painted wrought-iron gates, dates from 1927 and is a notable landmark along the river.

NOTTINGHAM, THE ARCH OF REMEMBRANCE, VICTORIA EMBANKMENT 1928 81563

Nottingham has begun the 21st century by bringing back an old form of transport - trams - which give a distinctly Continental air to the city streets.

NOTTINGHAM, THE STATUE OF ROBIN HOOD c1955 N50090

In the 14th and 15th centuries one of Nottingham's local industries was the carving of alabaster ornaments.

Nottingham's famous Goose Fair, which for centuries was held in the Market Place, may have originally been held in Weekday Cross. It is a matter of conjecture how old the fair is, but tradition states that it dates from 1284, the year of the charter of Edward I. As with many fairs, Nottingham's fair took place after harvest time, when the geese had been fattened on the corn stubble. The fair was originally intended as a market, but during the 20th century it became a pleasure fair.

For hundreds of years the names of Robin Hood and Nottingham have been inseparably linked, yet it was not until 1952, through the generosity of Nottingham businessman Philip Clay, that the city acquired a statue of its most famous character. It is positioned just outside Nottingham Castle walls (see page 28).

The recipe for the famous HP brown sauce was invented by a Nottingham shopkeeper, F G Garton. He called his sauce HP as he heard that it was being served in a restaurant in the Houses of Parliament. Unfortunately Mr Garton failed to make his fortune with HP sauce, as he sold the recipe and brand name for £150 to settle a debt.

There had been a small tobacco factory in Nottingham for over 50 years when John Player took it over in 1877, but it was in the late 1890s that the great expansion in the business took place which led in 1901 to the foundation of the Imperial Tobacco Company.

The Raleigh Cycle Company was founded in Nottingham by Frank Bowden, who in 1887 invested in a small bicycle works and within a few years had created the world's largest bicycle factory. James Samuel Archer, the co-inventor of the famous Sturmey-Archer three-speed bicycle gears, lived in Nottingham and worked at the Raleigh Cycle Company.

Park Steps (see page 31) was an ancient path between Lenton and Nottingham. The steps were cut when the Duke of Newcastle began to develop the Park Estate in 1829. They lead from Park Valley to the Ropewalk.

The Mother Church of Nottingham has the appearance, if not the stature, of a cathedral. Mentioned in the Domesday Book, the present building dates from the 15th century. The church was in danger of collapsing in the 19th century and was completely restored by Sir George Gilbert Scott and William Moffat.

NOTTINGHAM, PARK STEPS 1920 69433

NOTTINGHAM, THE FLYING HORSE HOTEL 1920 69427

The Flying Horse Hotel was one of the landmarks of Nottingham for many centuries and it is a matter of conjecture how it came by its name. The original building was Tudor, but it has a history of being rebuilt. In 1987 it was converted into a shopping arcade.

Until 1885 Wheeler Gate was a narrow street only wide enough for one vehicle to pass through at a time. The western side was then demolished and rebuilt, but it was another seven years before the eastern side was pulled down to give the road the width which exists today.

Nottingham's proximity to a navigable river that was also fordable has played a great part in the city's success. By the 20th century Nottingham was a major inland port with huge petrol tankers plying from Hull to Colwick. Since the decrease in the transport of goods by water, the growth in the leisure boat industry has given the river a new lease of life.

Nottingham's elegant suspension bridge over the River Trent was built in 1906, primarily to carry water pipes from Wilford Hill Reservoir to the Meadows, and also as a footbridge over the River Trent. The design of the two arches carrying the cables was matched in the 1920s when the Arch of Remembrance to the dead of the First World War was built nearby.

NOTTINGHAM, THE SUSPENSION BRIDGE c1950 N50303

Captain Albert Ball, VC was a great flying ace of the First World War; he was killed in action at the age of 20. It was suggested that this statue (below) should be sculpted by Auguste Rodin, but he declined, and the work was executed by Henry Poole.

NOTTINGHAM,
THE STATUE OF ALBERT BALL 1923 74598

William Booth, the founder of the Salvation Army, was born at 12 Notintone Place in Nottingham in 1829.

NOTTINGHAM, THE MARKET PLACE 1890 22809

In this view (above) of the Market Place the Exchange can be seen in the background. This building was designed in 1724 by the mayor, Marmaduke Pennel, and was built for the cost of £2,400; it was largely rebuilt in 1814. Among the many rooms used for public purposes was a very large one referred to as the ballroom. Underneath the Exchange and facing the Market Place were four shops, whilst most of the ground floor was taken up by the butchers' stalls, known as the Shambles. The Exchange was demolished in 1926 when the Council House was built.

Nottingham Goose Fair is held in Nottingham for three days every October. In its heyday as a hiring fair and autumn market for the Midlands it is estimated that up to 20,000 geese changed hands each year at the fair.

The first bridge over the Trent was built around 920 by Edward the Elder, the son of Alfred the Great. This had stone piers on oak piles and was replaced in 1156 by a second bridge known as the Hethbethebrigg - there is no definitive spelling of the name and the meaning of this word is unclear. Like most bridges of its time Trent Bridge had its own chapel; in 1303 a charity was formed to provide two chaplains to celebrate divine service daily, 'for the souls of all Christians who assigned goods to the maintenance of this bridge'.

In the photograph below we can see A J Witty's pleasure steamers 'Sunbeam' and 'Queen' at Turney's Quay. River trips became so popular that a third vessel was required, the 'Empress', which was also built at Witty's boatyard. The 'Empress' was sunk in 1940 while on its second crossing to Dunkirk during the evacuation from France.

NOTTINGHAM, TRENT BRIDGE 1902 48328

James Hargreaves introduced his Spinning Jenny machine into a small spinning mill off Lower Parliament Street in 1767, after escaping to Nottingham from Lancashire, where his machine had been wrecked by weavers worried that it would affect their jobs. In 1771 Richard Arkwright also set up his first spinning mill in Nottingham. These were both defining moments in the Industrial Revolution, but came at great cost to the thriving cottage industry

NOTTINGHAM, OLD MARKET SQUARE c1950 N50054

that already existed. The cottagers could not compete against the new machines in the industrial mills, and in desperation many of them banded together to destroy them. The gangs became known as Luddites, after their (probably imaginary) leader Ned Ludd. Although Luddism spread throughout the north of England during the early days of industrialisation, many people believe that the movement began in Nottingham.

NOTTINGHAM, MARKET SQUARE 1923 74594

SPORTING NOTTINGHAM

Two football clubs have their grounds in or near Nottingham: Nottingham Forest, and Notts County, the oldest Football League club in the country. Although Nottingham Forest FC's ground is called the City Ground it is not in the City of Nottingham but at West Bridgford. Notts County FC's ground is in the City of Nottingham, on Meadow Lane.

November 1947 saw a football transfer which could surely never happen today. Tommy Lawton, one of the top players of the day, and an England international, joined Notts County for a British record fee. County were in Division Three at the time. It was a sensational move, and caused over 45,000 people to attend the Boxing Day fixture against Swansea. Lawton is widely regarded as the best player ever to play for the club.

Test Match cricket is played Notts County Cricket Ground, generally known as Trent Bridge, with the City of Nottingham on one side and West Bridgford on the other. A particularly notable match at Trent bridge was one between England and Australia on 1-3 June 1899. It was the first game of the first ever 5-match series between the countries. Perhaps the most interesting fact concerns the age of the players. W G Grace was playing his last England match at the age of 50 years, 320 days. Coincidentally, a player making his England debut in the match, Wilfred Rhodes, was later to become the only other player to appear for England when over the age of 50.

Nottingham Forest FC was born out of a group of players of a game called 'shinney', a popular 19th-century game similar to hockey. In 1865 the shinney players decided to form a football club, and Forest came into being. They called themselves 'Nottingham Forest' because they played on the Forest Recreation Ground. Their early years were marked by a number of 'firsts'. They were the first English team to wear shinguards. They also played in the first game where a referee's whistle was used. Most importantly from a football point of view, they are credited with inventing, under the leadership of Sam Widdowson, the classic football combination of the fullbacks, three halfbacks, and five forwards, the formation which was almost universal for more than 50 years.

Brian Clough OBE is regarded by many football fans as the greatest manager in the history of football. He managed Nottingham Forest from 1975 until 1993, and led the club to two European Cup wins, and two League championships.

QUIZ QUESTIONS

Answers on page 49.

1. At the Peace of Wedmore in AD 878 (between the Danes and King Alfred the Great), Nottingham was absorbed into the 'Danelaw' (the area under Danish/Viking control) as one of the Five Boroughs. Which other towns were included in the Five Boroughs?

2. By what complimentary name is Nottingham sometimes known?

3. In which year was Nottingham awarded city status?

4. What ghastly event took place at Nottingham Castle in 1212?

5. In 1983 the ice skaters Torvill and Dean premiered their famous 'Bolero' routine at the British Championships at Nottingham. They went on to win the gold medal at the 1984 Sarajevo Winter Olympic Games with an unprecedented maximum score. What was the profession of Christopher Dean before he took up skating full time?

6. Why did King Richard III call Nottingham Castle his 'Castle of Care'?

7. He was born and bred in Nottingham; he began his football career with Arsenal; in his second season with Newcastle he scored 34 goals; on signing to Manchester United he broke the British transfer fee record, costing £6.25 million; he won the European 'Golden Boot' and PFA Young Player of the Year award in 1994; he has won Premier League, FA Cup and Champions League medals. Not bad for a Nottingham boy! Who is he?

8. Nottingham Forest won the FA Cup in 1959, 2-1 against Luton Town. The first Reds goal was scored by Roy Dwight, who broke his leg in a tackle half an hour later and had to watch the rest of the game on television from his hospital bed. Who is Roy Dwight's famous cousin?

9. A Nottinghamshire player was the first cricket player to score a 'cricketer's double' - 100 wickets and 1,000 runs - in the 1883 season. Who was he?

10. According to local legend, what was the reason that caused William Lee of Nottingham in 1685 to invent the framework knitting machine which revolutionised Nottingham's lacemaking industry?

NOTTINGHAM, PELHAM STREET 1890 22823

RECIPE

NOTTINGHAM PUDDING

The Bramley cooking apple originates from Southwell, a small minster town a short distance from Nottingham.

6 even-sized Bramley apples

3oz/75g butter

3oz/75g soft brown sugar

Nutmeg

Cinnamon

6 tablespoons (approx 6oz/175g) plain flour

Water

3 eggs

Salt

Milk (approx ¾ pint/450ml)

Peel and core the apples. Cream the butter and sugar, and add a good pinch each of nutmeg and cinnamon. Fill the centre of each apple with the mixture. Place in a well-buttered oven-proof dish. Blend the flour with a little cold water and add the well-beaten eggs to it with a pinch of salt and sufficient milk to make a thick creamy batter. Pour over the apples and bake at Gas Mark 6/400 degrees F/200 degrees C for 50 minutes.

NOTTINGHAM, CARRINGTON STREET 1890 22819

NOTTINGHAM, MARKET SQUARE 1923 74594

RECIPE

TRADITIONAL ROAST GOOSE

Nottingham is famous for its Goose Fair.

1 goose (complete with giblets)
4oz/115g pork
4oz/115g veal
1 large onion
Small knob of butter
2 slices of bread soaked in milk
1 egg yolk
Parsley, thyme, sage, finely chopped
3fl oz/75ml red wine

Chop the pork, veal, onion and the goose liver very finely and brown them in the butter. Squeeze the milk out of the bread and mix together all the ingredients except the wine, and using only a little of the wine to moisten. Season with salt and pepper to taste. Stuff the goose and put into a very hot oven, about 450 degrees F/230 degrees C/Gas Mark 8, for fifteen minutes. Reduce heat to 350 degrees F/180 degrees C/Gas Mark 4, and cook for fifteen minutes per lb/450g, basting with the remaining wine.

NOTTINGHAM, TRENT BRIDGE 1902 48329

QUIZ ANSWERS

1. The other towns in the Five Boroughs were Stamford, Leicester, Lincoln and nearby Derby.
2. Nottingham is known by many as 'The Queen of the Midlands'.
3. Nottingham was awarded city status in 1897.
4. In 1212 King John hanged 28 Welsh boy hostages from Nottingham Castle walls during a Welsh rebellion.
5. Christopher Dean was formerly a policeman in Nottingham.
6. This name does not, as popularly supposed, reflect King Richard's melancholy view of the castle, but quite the opposite - a modern rendering might be 'the castle of his regard and care', as he was very fond of Nottingham Castle.
7. Andy Cole.
8. The pop star Elton John, whose real name is Reg Dwight.
9. Wilfred Flowers, who played for Nottinghamshire (between 1877-96) and England (eight times, including two tours to Australia).
10. The story says that he was courting a local girl who spent so much time knitting that he got the idea of inventing a mechanised knitting machine to allow them to spend more time together.

NOTTINGHAM, LONG ROW EAST 1890 22814

NOTTINGHAM, THE SCHOOL OF ART 1890 24708

FRANCIS FRITH

PIONEER VICTORIAN PHOTOGRAPHER

Francis Frith, founder of the world-famous photographic archive, was a complex and multi-talented man. A devout Quaker and a highly successful Victorian businessman, he was philosophical by nature and pioneering in outlook. By 1855 he had already established a wholesale grocery business in Liverpool, and sold it for the astonishing sum of £200,000, which is the equivalent today of over £15,000,000. Now in his thirties, and captivated by the new science of photography, Frith set out on a series of pioneering journeys up the Nile and to the Near East.

INTRIGUE AND EXPLORATION

He was the first photographer to venture beyond the sixth cataract of the Nile. Africa was still the mysterious 'Dark Continent', and Stanley and Livingstone's historic meeting was a decade into the future. The conditions for picture taking confound belief. He laboured for hours in his wicker dark-room in the sweltering heat of the desert, while the volatile chemicals fizzed dangerously in their trays. Back in London he exhibited his photographs and was 'rapturously cheered' by members of the Royal Society. His reputation as a photographer was made overnight.

VENTURE OF A LIFE-TIME

By the 1870s the railways had threaded their way across the country, and Bank Holidays and half-day Saturdays had been made obligatory by Act of Parliament. All of a sudden the working man and his family were able to enjoy days out, take holidays, and see a little more of the world.

With typical business acumen, Francis Frith foresaw that these new tourists would enjoy having souvenirs to commemorate their days out. For the next thirty years he travelled the country by train and by pony and trap, producing fine photographs of seaside resorts and beauty spots that were keenly bought by millions of Victorians. These prints were painstakingly pasted into family albums and pored over during the dark nights of winter, rekindling precious memories of summer excursions. Frith's studio was soon supplying retail shops all over the country, and by 1890 F Frith & Co had become the greatest specialist photographic publishing company in the world, with over 2,000 sales outlets, and pioneered the picture postcard.

FRANCIS FRITH'S LEGACY

Francis Frith had died in 1898 at his villa in Cannes, his great project still growing. By 1970 the archive he created contained over a third of a million pictures showing 7,000 British towns and villages.

Frith's legacy to us today is of immense significance and value, for the magnificent archive of evocative photographs he created provides a unique record of change in the cities, towns and villages throughout Britain over a century and more. Frith and his fellow studio photographers revisited locations many times down the years to update their views, compiling for us an enthralling and colourful pageant of British life and character.

We are fortunate that Frith was dedicated to recording the minutiae of everyday life. For it is this sheer wealth of visual data, the painstaking chronicle of changes in dress, transport, street layouts, buildings, housing and landscape that captivates us so much today, offering us a powerful link with the past and with the lives of our ancestors.

Computers have now made it possible for Frith's many thousands of images to be accessed almost instantly. The archive offers every one of us an opportunity to examine the places where we and our families have lived and worked down the years. Its images, depicting our shared past, are now bringing pleasure and enlightenment to millions around the world a century and more after his death.

For further information visit: www.francisfrith.com

INTERIOR DECORATION

Frith's photographs can be seen framed and as giant wall murals in thousands of pubs, restaurants, hotels, banks, retail stores and other public buildings throughout Britain. These provide interesting and attractive décor, generating strong local interest and acting as a powerful reminder of gentler days in our increasingly busy and frenetic world.

FRITH PRODUCTS

All Frith photographs are available as prints and posters in a variety of different sizes and styles. In the UK we also offer a range of other gift and stationery products illustrated with Frith photographs, although many of these are not available for delivery outside the UK – see our web site for more information on the products available for delivery in your country.

THE INTERNET

Over 100,000 photographs of Britain can be viewed and purchased on the Frith web site. The web site also includes memories and reminiscences contributed by our customers, who have personal knowledge of localities and of the people and properties depicted in Frith photographs. If you wish to learn more about a specific town or village you may find these reminiscences fascinating to browse. Why not add your own comments if you think they would be of interest to others? See **www.francisfrith.com**

PLEASE HELP US BRING FRITH'S PHOTOGRAPHS TO LIFE

Our authors do their best to recount the history of the places they write about. They give insights into how particular towns and villages developed, they describe the architecture of streets and buildings, and they discuss the lives of famous people who lived there. But however knowledgeable our authors are, the story they tell is necessarily incomplete.

Frith's photographs are so much more than plain historical documents. They are living proofs of the flow of human life down the generations. They show real people at real moments in history; and each of those people is the son or daughter of someone, the brother or sister, aunt or uncle, grandfather or grandmother of someone else. All of them lived, worked and played in the streets depicted in Frith's photographs.

We would be grateful if you would give us your insights into the places shown in our photographs: the streets and buildings, the shops, businesses and industries. Post your memories of life in those streets on the Frith website: what it was like growing up there, who ran the local shop and what shopping was like years ago; if your workplace is shown tell us about your working day and what the building is used for now. Read other visitors' memories and reconnect with your shared local history and heritage. With your help more and more Frith photographs can be brought to life, and vital memories preserved for posterity, and for the benefit of historians in the future.

Wherever possible, we will try to include some of your comments in future editions of our books. Moreover, if you spot errors in dates, titles or other facts, please let us know, because our archive records are not always completely accurate—they rely on 140 years of human endeavour and hand-compiled records. You can email us using the contact form on the website.

Thank you!

For further information, trade, or author enquiries
please contact us at the address below:

The Francis Frith Collection, 6 Oakley Business Park, Wylye Road, Dinton, Wiltshire SP3 5EU.

Tel: +44 (0)1722 716 376 Fax: +44 (0)1722 716 881
e-mail: sales@francisfrith.co.uk **www.francisfrith.com**

FRITH PRODUCTS & SERVICES

Francis Frith would doubtless be pleased to know that the pioneering publishing venture he started in 1860 still continues today. Over a hundred and forty years later, The Francis Frith Collection continues in the same innovative tradition and is now one of the foremost publishers of vintage photographs in the world. Some of the current activities include:

INTERIOR DECORATION

Today Frith's photographs can be seen framed and as giant wall murals in thousands of pubs, restaurants, hotels, banks, retail stores and other public buildings throughout the country. In every case they enhance the unique local atmosphere of the places they depict and provide reminders of gentler days in an increasingly busy and frenetic world.

PRODUCT PROMOTIONS

Frith products are used by many major companies to promote the sales of their own products or to reinforce their own history and heritage. Frith promotions have been used by Hovis bread, Courage beers, Scots Porage Oats, Colman's mustard, Cadbury's foods, Mellow Birds coffee, Dunhill pipe tobacco, Guinness, and Bulmer's Cider.

GENEALOGY AND FAMILY HISTORY

As the interest in family history and roots grows world-wide, more and more people are turning to Frith's photographs of Great Britain for images of the towns, villages and streets where their ancestors lived; and, of course, photographs of the churches and chapels where their ancestors were christened, married and buried are an essential part of every genealogy tree and family album.

FRITH PRODUCTS

All Frith photographs are available Framed or just as Mounted Prints and unmounted versions. These may be ordered from the address below. Other products available are - Calendars, Jigsaws, Canvas Prints, Mugs, Tea Towels, Tableware and local and prestige books.

THE INTERNET

Over several hundred thousand Frith photographs can be viewed and purchased on the internet through the Frith websites!

For more detailed information on Frith products, look at www.francisfrith.com

See the complete list of Frith Books at: www.francisfrith.com

This web site is regularly updated with the latest list of publications from The Francis Frith Collection. If you wish to buy books relating to another part of the country that your local bookshop does not stock, you may purchase on-line.

For further information, trade, or author enquiries please contact us at the address below:

The Francis Frith Collection, 19 Kingsmead Business Park, Gillingham, Dorset SP8 5FB.

Tel: +44 (0)1722 716 376 Email: sales@francisfrith.co.uk

See Frith products on the internet at www.francisfrith.com

FREE PRINT OF YOUR CHOICE
CHOOSE A PHOTOGRAPH FROM THIS BOOK

+ POSTAGE

Mounted Print
Overall size 14 x 11 inches (355 x 280mm)

TO RECEIVE YOUR FREE PRINT

Choose any Frith photograph in this book

Simply complete the Voucher opposite and return it with your payment (to cover postage and handling) and we will print the photograph of your choice in SEPIA (size 11 x 8 inches) and supply it in a cream mount ready to frame (overall size 14 x 11 inches).

Order additional Mounted Prints at HALF PRICE - £19.00 each (normally £38.00)

If you would like to order more Frith prints from this book, possibly as gifts for friends and family, you can buy them at half price (with no additional postage costs).

Have your Mounted Prints framed

For an extra £20.00 per print you can have your mounted print(s) framed in an elegant polished wood and gilt moulding, overall size 16 x 13 inches (no additional postage required).

IMPORTANT!

❶ Please note: aerial photographs and photographs with a reference number starting with a "Z" are not Frith photographs and cannot be supplied under this offer.

❷ Offer valid for delivery to one UK address only.

❸ These special prices are only available if you use this form to order. You must use the ORIGINAL VOUCHER on this page (no copies permitted). We can only despatch to one UK address.

❹ This offer cannot be combined with any other offer.

As a customer your name & address will be stored by Frith but not sold or rented to third parties. Your data will be used for the purpose of this promotion only.

Send completed Voucher form to:

The Francis Frith Collection,
19 Kingsmead Business Park, Gillingham,
Dorset SP8 5FB

Voucher *for FREE and Reduced Price Frith Prints*

Please do not photocopy this voucher. Only the original is valid, so please fill it in, cut it out and return it to us with your order.

Picture ref no	Page no	Qty	Mounted @ £19.00	Framed + £20.00	Total Cost £
		1	Free of charge*	£	£
			£19.00	£	£
			£19.00	£	£
			£19.00	£	£
			£19.00	£	£
			£19.00	£	£
			* Post & handling		£3.80
			Total Order Cost		£

Please allow 28 days for delivery.
Offer available to one UK address only

Title of this book ....
I enclose a cheque/postal order for £ ....
made payable to 'The Francis Frith Collection'

OR please debit my Mastercard / Visa / Maestro card, details below

Card Number:

Issue No (Maestro only): Valid from (Maestro):

Card Security Number: Expires:

Signature:

Name Mr/Mrs/Ms ....
Address ....
....
....
.... Postcode ....
Daytime Tel No ....
Email ....

Valid to 31/12/20

Free Print - see overleaf

Can you help us with information about any of the Frith photographs in this book?

We are gradually compiling an historical record for each of the photographs in the Frith archive. It is always fascinating to find out the names of the people shown in the pictures, as well as insights into the shops, buildings and other features depicted.

If you recognize anyone in the photographs in this book, or if you have information not already included in the author's caption, do let us know. We would love to hear from you, and will try to publish it in future books or articles.

An Invitation from The Francis Frith Collection to Share Your Memories

The 'Share Your Memories' feature of our website allows members of the public to add personal memories relating to the places featured in our photographs, or comment on others already added. Seeing a place from your past can rekindle forgotten or long held memories. Why not visit the website, find photographs of places you know well and add YOUR story for others to read and enjoy? We would love to hear from you!

www.francisfrith.com/memories

Our production team

Frith books are produced by a small dedicated team at offices near Salisbury. Most have worked with the Frith Collection for many years. All have in common one quality: they have a passion for the Frith Collection.

Frith Books and Gifts

We have a wide range of books and gifts available on our website utilising our photographic archive, many of which can be individually personalised.

www.francisfrith.com